Hotel Gwales

Nigel Jenkins

Gomer

First Impression – 2006

ISBN 1 84323 663 X
ISBN-13 9781843236634

© Nigel Jenkins

This book is published with the financial support
of the Welsh Books Council.

*Printed in Wales at
Gomer Press, Llandysul, Ceredigion SA44 4JL*

To my mother, Gloria,
in the year of her 80th birthday,
with love.

ACKNOWLEDGEMENTS

Acknowledgements are due to the editors of the following, in which some of these poems first appeared: *Between a Mountain and a Sea*, *Cambria*, *English Journal* (U.S.A.), *In een ander licht* (Netherlands), *Kritya* (India; www.kritya.org), *Planet*, *Poetry Now Anthology 1999* (Ireland), *Poetry Wales*, *Scintilla*, *The Bloodaxe Book of Modern Welsh Poetry* (2003), *The Bucks County Writer* (U.S.A.), *The New Welsh Review*, *Sampler*, *Slope* (U.S.A; www.slope.org/archive/eight/main.html). 'A Body of Questions' was published as a six-face chap-sheet by the Red Pagoda Press, Pennsylvania, U.S.A.

I would like to thank Menna Elfyn, Iwan Llwyd and Ifor ap Glyn for permission to republish my translations of their poems, and I am grateful to Osi Rhys Osmond for the cover photograph of his work 'Cwch Manawydan' in the *Fenws Machynlleth* series.

CONTENTS

HANDBOOK

From anti-void to supernovae,
from the mating of matter
to the rebirth of seas
and the invention of gods,

it has come down to this,
this callus grown
on a fleeting finger
from the daily struggle

to unearth, perhaps, a word or two.

★

If the hand has written everything,
every thing has written the hand.

★

Alone or cupped together
– for nuts, blackberries, water, sand –
you reinvent, daily,
the first bowl,

and could spill, no doubt,
a bean or two
pertaining to the second,

a slice of blood-tight cranium.

★

And then the thumb,
cruising above the prairies of the palm
and docking tip-to-tip with
one finger after another,

achieved fecund opposition,

sparking speech, circles,
straight and sometimes bloody lines.

★

Though you've come a long way, hands,
from those invocatory savannas
you have not forgotten

the padding of palms
upon waterless earth,

or a notion, among trees,
of fruit that might not be

unreachable.

★

Branch, stick;
          stick, club:
handy how
– with the grip you achieved
as you climbed those trees –
you invented killing,

though aeons would pass
before you came

to discover death.

★

You built nests, gathered fruit,
scratched the head as you fumbled,

fumbled for stooped millennia
at those exclusive hides,

until you were minded
to breed from two stones
the blade that set you striding
through valleys of meat,

on your way, with scalpel,
to the brain.

★

Striking stone, you struck fire,
striking fire, you struck the voice
that called hand unto hand

to bring meat to its knees

and to articulate,
even of tundra,
a homely country.

★

Knapping stone,
felling mammoth,
plucking leaves,
piking roach,
scraping skins,
cupping berries,
sewing hides,
dragging wood,
fretting fire,
spitting meat,

harvesting the time

11

to start work
on this poem.

★

Hand to mouth,
fruit by fruit,
grain by grain,
the palm always, at last,
lethally empty –

until the idea
of tomorrow took root:

the hand that then put by one seed
had plans – temptatious rhyme – for greed.

★

The arm, a trunk;
the fingers, five branches;

the deeds of those fingers

blown leaves blown
where there's world to see them.

★

Lately this itch, this itch to crawl
far into the deepest deep of a mountain,
to distil there in paint
the wind-winged, essential herds,

this persistent itch, embellishing a spaceship
with patient blueprint of an open hand,
to catapult pictures into the dark.

12

★

Hand after hand
from dawntime falling
to the bed of clay,

until there come the fingers
– collapsing horizons, eroding the dark –
that carve in tablets of aluminous earth
intelligence that flies
from tomorrow to tomorrow.

What say you, death?
What say you now
to the hand of anon?

★

The escape from gravity:
to be up there in the tree,
dreaming hands into wing-tips;

to be out there in space,
a Voyager cargoed
with multilingual, sempiternal ads

that say much of the fingers,
little of the fist.

★

For each firm-hearted cabbage,
every trove of spuds, he gives
thanks to his hands.

Praise of god he saves

for the useless rose,
celestial handiwork
that brings him already
close to heaven.

★

The fist that kills a fly
(and writes the fly into this poem),
the index licked
for honey or snow,
the nail dark with whose menses –

the public, the private, the secret
lives of hands:
if people and police
knew the half of their tale

it would be
flee-from-me and handcuff time.

★

Through priestly Chaos they reached,
the Mediterranean fingers
of farmers, sailors, shipwrights, weavers,
to fathom the irreducible atom,
opening the eye
to the godless, holy music of Cosmos.

But the hand on the tiller
is lately of half a chaotic mind, proud
that in its pride the in-
divisible has been divided,
and dithering unto omnideath
'twixt fission and fusion,

14

as Cosmos awaits
              if not us
                    then others.

★

There are special rooms,
rooms for the fist

that are full of questions,
hair and blood,

rooms constructed
by hands never held,

by bodies and lives
uncaressed.

★

The back of my hand:
I know nothing if I don't know
these sinewed and latticed
fourteen square inches, their
sunned hairs as countable as stars.

But there has been this night,
and whose hand is this
that tells no tale
about the scratchmarks
smearing stubbed knuckles –

where even is the star of day?

★

You, who drive in your cars
to gaze at the ocean,
whose blood's chemistry echoes the sea's –

don't you find suggestive
that unemployed web
'twixt finger and thumb?

★

She told me how
a red and smaller-than-a-pinhead
spider, shy at first
of the warmth of her hand, had
climbed up onto
her index finger and
legs a-fizz
– though she'd felt not a thing –
set a knuckle-ward course.
Such then such
the insistent sunlight
boring pink passage
through the nose-flesh of her cat –
but she'd not dared the distraction
for fear of smearing
the scarlet traveller
through the blonde treescape.
So with one mouth-blast she
blew him clear,
though she has long wondered
how and whether he survived
that fall to concrete
of a metre or more.

★

Blessed the hand, desire willing,
that recovers, at night, between parted thighs

a way back to the sea
when love swam with unhated love

and fingers were fins.

★

Souvenirs of cooking and love –
the smell on my fingers
of garlic, of desire's lubricious liqueur . . .

oases, oceans filling my day.

★

How does it happen, the estranging of hands
that hunted, once, the tablecloths in pairs,
voracious for the touch
that liberates lips and closes eyes,

hands that when parted
would roll between four fingerless palms
the thirst of continents, the hunger of seas?

How does it happen
that these hands that felt their way
to a body's soul
would no more reach for those now

than seek their ease in acid or flame?

★

Nothing bigger, once,
than this fist-crushed can
at the water's edge.

★

We watched and we listened to
the work of his hands: he drugged us
with blues and the blues drugged him

with money, women, narcotic fame

until he and his albatross
seemed at last
to disappear from his life.

His remains, years later, were shown
on TV: a jobless recluse,
with every fingernail grown
a twirling foot long,

that no guitar
would ever again
sneak its way into those claws.

★

Have you noticed how clean,
when he hands you your change,

are the butcher's hands?

★

She is the latest to discover,
in how many more than a million years,
that her hand composes

the perfect cup for her baby's head.

★

An orderly hand takes
a measured shuffle

across the page,
making note, for some reason,

of yon red tower
and the uncle who had
to spend a lifetime there,

a hand disinclined
to blood with burden
of its own ravened nails

the immaculate square.

★

Reopen the wound, that half-inch of white
aslant the thumb's splayed mons,
nothing to be ashamed of, the left's
blood bombing the chemicalized earth,
just a slip of the right, secateurs mis-angled
to snip not a grapestalk but crunchy flesh.

The scar recalls only the best of times
– *vin rouge* by the bucket, agricultural feeds,
the workers rewarded with each others' bodies –
of which the cicada,
secateured neatly, legs thrashing, in two,
is but the least of green and yellow things.

★

These veins tonight, these
lumpy back-roads
snaking the handscape,
how close they press
to murderous airlight,

19

how easy it would be
to visit them.

★

If I seem sometimes
to have the backs plumbed,

what scant attention
– unsold on hocus-pocus –
have I paid to the palms;
though so much closer to the action,
they seem sometimes another story.

But I've only to look to my dreams to know
that in this hand that has never hit a child

a monster sleeps.

★

My father's hands, in death's labours,
would toil at his brow
as if in the hayfield
his father and his father
were swiping sweat and seeds
from a yawning head.

What turns of hand
are dealt by sperm and ovum?
The killing I want done these days
is work for hired hands,
but would I slit a throat of duck
or the gullet of a Norman
with a familial touch
perhaps borne in the bone
from Cro-Magnon times?

– though younger by aeons
than the hand of all my fathers
that glides home to warm seas
along my lover's thigh.

★

Okay, okay, it's a right-handed world,
and don't we left-out lefties know it?
You've got it made, brother – 'tool of tools' –
from scissors to corkscrews, from nuts and bolts
to the zippers on flies; it's you that gets to open
doors for the ladies and the doors of ladies,
or to work the throbous rise of a cock;
yours the adroit and prestigious jobs
– look at you pushing that poet's pen –
while, sinister and gauche, 'the hand of the privy',
I get the unskilled, twilight chores. But if I can't so much
as peel a spud or sign this scribbler's name,
let me remind you, Mr Right is Might,
that mine is rarely the finger on the trigger.

★

The hand of power was extended
to the hand of power;
for a second or two
their palms united composed
a tiny galaxy awaiting stars –

and two peoples risked something
approaching a smile.

★

The hand on your shoulder
and the silence it keeps –

21

are you leading
or are you being led?

★

The soldier – as my splayed hand's
little finger and thumb
began to coax your nipple's rise –

the soldier amputee
who could still feel the pain
in his missing hands

would not be absented.

★

Out of touch with the world, straitjacketed
in shoes, we are seen, if seen at all,
as hands manqués, whiffy might-have-beens
whose digits could barely transport a twig,

good for no more than stomping a beat
as the fingers of Hendrix booglerize souls.

O maestro of the shoelace, we are
not such antipodean cousins:
until we stood and walked our ground
you too were a scuttle of thumbs.

Footloosened at last to finger into being
your prestidigitatory realms,
there are things of earth perhaps
you have misremembered –
humility, unison, the receipt of pleasure.

So, come, touch; reach down and touch:

this too – the toes a-splay,
the arching and curling – this too is transport.

★

It has been decided
by the most complicated object
in the known cosmos

that two fists will be made,
one of the left hand, one of the right,
and that these fists will be conjoined
knuckle to knuckle, wrist to wrist,
like two thoughtful hemispheres;

whereupon it has been further provided
that the faintest of smiles
may ghost the lips in celebration

of a simile's homage
to a working relationship

older than the first cupping of rain.

★

Having slept the sleep of white ocarinas,
the baby wakes: in those crystal coals

that no colour yet has dared to name
there is all and none of the world's story,

as old men drift through her
and star-flung dancers, many hands passing by,

fingering space, beginning slowly
to remember themselves.

23

HOTEL GWALES°

(for Lisa Glass)

There will be, there'll have to be
a table round as the rings of Sadwrn,
high-back chairs, marble columns and floors
and two oaken doors as high
as sky's blue and as wide as desire
on a sun-fizzing sea.

A cloud for a roof will keep us cool
and nothing shall we suffer
of the griefs we've seen
(unless the hand of unwisdom
opens door number three).
Nothing that's illegal
will need to be snorted
for all to be extraordinarily well.

Mare's-tail drapes will stir
in Moroccan zephyrs,
as Brad Mehldau makes free
on a gleaming black grand
and staff, disturbingly beautiful staff
sashay back and forth with food and drink
and tantalizing invitations
to eternal life.

Yes, all will be well
until sometime before even
a century's done
some bearded noser
flings wide – on guess what –
old door number three.

SOME LINES TO REQUEST POTEEN°

Praise, Terry, your ace poteen
and praise be that Neath's *heddlu*
are averse, no doubt, to verse –
we want no drug squad readers.
These dry lines, *cynghanedd*-free,
are sent to say I'm thirsty
for more of that cosmic juice
(spiritless bards are no use)
which, by the time I've finished
this, will have passed to the fish
of Swansea Bay, the bottle
ready to ferry this scrawl
across to Melincryddan's
spirit–maker number one.
Ice on fire, you're the poet
of where the contentions meet,
your wisdom's mirth an oak whorled
from the killing fields' antiworld
and your pained hands' outlaw love
for loves the world's afraid of.

It's late and getting later,
I'm a poet needs the fire
that only you can distil:
a Mumbler craves a refill.

Sláinte, then, and *iechyd da*
to Wales that voiced you, Eire
whose fatherly hand led you,
star by stream, to rebel muse
and old alchemical ways
with water, fire, fruit, barley.
Essence of unmachined rain,
most magical of moonshines,

clearer than ice and iced air,
though of suns the container;
exploder in the nostrils
of red orchards, dusty fields;
semen of the gods, hot blood
of goddesses, all falsehoods'
undressing when love defers
to the teachers and preachers;
song sprung from its silences
– bass of choirs, sky of pipes –
to set all atoms dancing,
the whole galaxy a-swing.
Each sip – and no 'head', thank god –
a fleadh cum wild eisteddfod.

The tide's in, the spirit's out:
be, Terry, on the look-out
for landfall on your doorstep
of this craft poteen-bereft,
barnacled and seaweed-draped
as proof of long, hard voyage,
weighed with verse and a bard's curse
on all hooch-busting peelers:
may every glass their thirsts crave
turn to boiling aftershave.
Here's a hope this plea finds you
stocked enough with cosmic brew
to save me from my drouth's hell
by filling full this vessel.
Hurl it then towards the stars
and I'll run from my boudoir
to catch it on re-entry,
Melin's gift to Mumbling me.
So pour, Ter, the nectar in
that's sure to set me writing
(light, *awen*, on this windbag!)
full *cynghanedd* – *yn Gymraeg*.

First and last I'll drink to you,
friend, bard and oaken guru.
Your spirit spells revival:
may your still be never still.

PUB DRUNK

He teeters along a vanishing line,
his brain a sog of blown connections,
locked, with vague and rapt intent,
on Point B: his balancing act
could be transporting a round for two,
though all he holds is his liquid self.

When it's time to go he
sails forth, fag aloft, towards the light,
his cigarette arm lowering, as his left grabs
the door, lowering as if in enfolding mode,
as if he were leaving – why not? – with a lover,
a blonde lover on his right arm.

ON THE EDUCATION OF
WELSH BUS DRIVERS°

(i.m. Dai Jones, 1944-2002)

Your lamb that night, Dai of the roads,
was a rack of aurochs, your fifty-eighth birthday
a bon viveur's Segontium reprieve
from the washed-out wettest of all our tours
that 'sooner or later had to happen . . .'
And has to happen: it was the day I'd decided,
to my silent self, that the spicule of 'bread'
stuck for weeks to my palate
was not benignly inclined to our Luxury Travels –
and the coach, next time, could be one of us less.

As the rain rained and the students snoozed
through my miked-up bookish dronery,
I'd tongue, between pearls, the ambitious blip
– that later proved nothing but a mucocele.
But I was right about at least
the unbearable future lightness of the Leyland's load.

'Bus man falls through depot roof' – and not all Demetia's
intensive care could keep your chariot on the pass.
Thousands are the eyes that scour in vain now
every cinammon-and-yellow Ffoshelig coach
for that hale and *haelionus*, joyous wave.
As highway robbed as the roads of Cymru
are the fields of Sir Gâr, the foxhunts, the choirs,
the point-to-points, the sports clubs, the *eisteddfodau*,
and the hedgepaths home to Mair and Fferm y Sarnau.

You would drive and I'd contrive
a wishful Wales, encyclopaedic Jenkins
booming strange facts to your startled ears.

'Ah well,' yawned once a sleepyhead,
'these trips must do something, if nothing else,
for the education of Welsh bus drivers.'

But the education of this bus driver,
who lived a Wales unsniffed by the books,
was a gift at day's end, with a Guinness, to me –
from the wanderings with dog
through fields of witness, to Gareth's lazy racer
shotgunned with corn, or the farewell to hounds
so's not to upset the *Saeson* who've moved in:
Cymru's hearted, incorrect and sacred life.
Skirting Fferm y Sarnau, journey's end in sight,
I can pass round only this hat of words
in salutation, Dai, of a hand still at the wheel
on this lethally whimsical mystery tour.

LLYWELYN AP GRUFFUDD FYCHAN°

We come, Llywelyn ap Gruffudd Fychan,
with our softened hands and the illusion
of a government we can call our own,
to piece back the pieces and rediscover you
whole, memory twining again with desire
to seed, against all common sense, the practical dream.

A day in October (I do not want to see it),
a day maybe of mountain rain, or a day perhaps
like the days you led the king and his lumbering army
up and down and round and round bewildering Deheubarth,
that your sons and Glyndŵr and the nation you were daring
might live to struggle a day, a week, six hundred years longer.
Or an autumn day (I do not want to see it)
as drowsy as a wasp at the gate of an apple, a perfect day
for an execution (I do not want to accept
the usurper king's unkind invitation).
War war war, sle sle sle the Welsh doggis and their whelps.
I do not want to witness the old father
bound, pistol-whipped and dragged to the gallows,
my eyes resist the advertised spectacle and main attraction
of that pale and pendulous gourmet's belly
knived at raggedly by the slaughterman's blade
till a gaping smile gives birth vomitous to oodling
screams unanimaled of earth, screams beyond
imagination's hearing, as men tickle, with talons of fire,
the steaming, soft machinery of his being.

Pour encourager les autres. The Empire starts here.
A good thrashing first – then, in the fullness of imperial time,
great kindness: bibles, railways, schools, TV . . .
I do not want to see on the news
the piked head, the torso loved of woman
quartered, salted, despatched as a warning to the four corners.

31

And what are we to make of the news?
Who the hero, who the villain? Is not war
a mutual atrocity? And were not the *uchelwyr*,
like as not, hawks and leeches on the lives beneath them?
If this man was loved, was he not rich?
And if rich Cymru's rich in hope in a ravened world
who is it, out of mind, that pays the price?

What we have made of the news is not what the king
would have us make, and we come, Llywelyn,
to piece back the pieces, to conjure home
your hatcheted limbs, to restore to those shoulders
your hazarding head and trickster smile, to wind those
blasphemed lights back within sound of your heart's *llan* –
and then in your right, unwavering hand
to settle a beaker of Gascony wine.

Your house, Llywelyn, is today a hill, and out of that hill
an oak rears, seismic with acorns: timber for ships, barrels, dreams –
for the hall you left us that's ours to complete.

'ROLL ON, THOU DEEP AND DARK BLUE OCEAN, ROLL!'°

Behold, where control and Aberystwyth end,
these Iowa farm girls gazing at the sea,

– never in all their land-locked lives –

minding, perhaps, the daddies they love, the moms
who'd be scared that way past midnight,
as their dragoman slept, their naked babies
had been midwinter skinny-dipping,
up to their tipsy scalps
in a black-seeming mirror of the disco-lit town.

My sea, their ocean

is not as it was, comes
clean this morning, comes and comes
with a churned, submarine, complex intent
that sunlight finds them, in Gore-Tex and woollens,
dressed to face: four Iowa farm girls, an acre apart,
gazing as from space to oceaned Earth,

and their guide – the bus leaves in ten minutes –
their guide, at the rail, gazing at them.

BINOCULAR

From high upon this hill
the scene down there
is not one
of wasps, ice creams,
cigars, Radio One and Brummies whining
as a cussing husband casts off in his yacht –

but of white sails

inclining with hope
against a grey conspiracy of sky and sea.

COAL

White world, grey endless sky —
the birds hunched and starving,
     our pipes frozen.

Of the sun there is nothing.

Yet when I scoop up
some snow, when I take in my hand
a coal fallen from the heaped bucket
I balance on my palm
the history of rivers, I am in touch
with dark original forests.

Branches of coal
spread out beneath us,

a language of the sun,
     locked
     by the ancient trees in their cells,
and translated again
     by the green sun
     that goes whispering
     through sinew and bone.

With deadened fingers
we build up the grate.

Seedlings of flame

shift and flicker: fire awakening,
fire remembering in its first tongue
the journey from sun to greening earth.

It fills up our faces,
and the rivers of cold
chase through our bodies

to spill from chasms just north
of the base of the spine.

DUSK AT THE QUEEN'S

Sundowner. Great beams of the hot stuff
shout down through the Queen's
high bowed panes, unreceived

by the bigshots and slinkies, lush
Dafydd on his back in a clearing of legs
– 'which way, Iesu mawr, which way is up?' –

the Sultans, the swing, the
love deals fixed and a spat raging
when – what the hell? – there hales in at the door

an old comrade of the vine
who stands to deliver, in a lull between discs,
an intelligence hot from his own front line.

'Appertaining,' he says, stubble to the stucco
as the wisechat wanes . . .
'Appertaining to the per-pen-dic-ular . . .

. . . I have nothing further to say –'
and he bangs back out, our eyes now ushered
to the street, the sky: this airborne thing, an

ambitious umbrella – no – a cormorant sailing
the officious length of Gloucester Place,
dusting all with silence as she scrapes the moon.

ON FOUR PAINTINGS
OF EVAN WALTERS

1. SELF-PORTRAIT WITH CANDLE

We have two of everything here
– don't we? – two of everything here . . .
The Artist, capital 'A', at binocular war
with *that dull robot the camera*,
the beret's black halo,
the 'tache of office and tuft imperial
declaring for Art and daring
– with two candles twiced –
to conjure such fire
as to pale the sun's paling
of his right that is not his right cheek.
You'd need a mirror to unmirror him,
to find palette and brush in left hand
while the right, off stage,
works its restless, incendiary magic.
From the revolution they will not buy,
he will not, the eyes insist, be deflected –
not by critics, curators, Mam o Nedd herself,
though the robot within
has long concealed a counter plan,
has long concealed a counter plan.

2. BOY WITH A FEATHER

it is

it is as if

it is as if
gravity itself

'twixt fingers as if
and lips as if

were in

suspension

3. REAR ADMIRAL WALKER-HENEAGE-VIVIAN

It comes down, the eye comes down
past ribbons, medals, tassels, stars
and almighty sleeves
to those fingerly bones
and that democratic cigarette –

and then returns
to the eyes at blue sea and the wreckage
of a smile.

The master, Walters, of *HMS Powerful*
has not got all day: there are
pheasants to be shot, communists to quell,
daughters to be avoided, and, above all,
rhododendrons to raise.

If a fag ain't the sum
of the Admiral's joys,
he will draw small delight
from this dauber's lurid dabs
as imperium's peacock cries its last,

though they're the best, if not all,
that will one day remain.

4. THE ARTIST'S MOTHER ASLEEP

There, he has said it, dared in paint to say
what the sleeping mother's son won't have said.
The son watches for the stertor to wane,
a gummy smile to sink that shark-snout head
as he brings her just a half cup of *cawl*.
She breathes, breathes still, who for son and painter
black-leaded the grate, kneaded dough, plucked fowl,
hallowed the language, affirmed the scriptures,
and once, for art – to *drws nesa*'s alarm –
took most of a morning to peg out one sheet.
Though the son has hedged her with orbic charms,
the painter, who has heard the stertor cease,
has created of the bed that bred him
his mother's iron and his own coffin.

ONCE UPON A TIME°

(for Branwen)

Come, as the whitebeam, come Bran again
to the big old bed, and I will
read to you while the silvering wind,
and you, Bran, will read to me,
Dad a page, then Bran a page.
From this 'rock of Harddlech overlooking
the sea' there are ships to be seen,
and in the blue beyond, arrivals of blood –
though may fiction's door preserve
our pillowed heads from tragedy's lethal absolutes.
Can you hear what I can hear
way across the years, those pigeons hallooing
a dawn brazen with the so much still
that was left to come? Do you hear now
this owl of a wind that will bring us soon,
until perhaps again, the last of leaves?
As birth's trumpets forefanfare a death,
so first smiles, first words, first christmases
are invisibly murmurous of the last.
There's no sitting any more on Daddy's knee,
and soon enough, your hand, like your sister's,
will banish mine on the school-pally streets.
So come, Bran, again to the bed that bred you,
we've a book to get read, you take the right page,
I'll take the left, and in the name of all
the Branwens who've been happy
we'll not open yet any Cornwall-facing doors.
The day will come, I know, when you'll
fly without your redundant co-reader,
but for now I am with you in griefless Gwales,
ready, when you yawn, to dog-ear a page
until – wait 'n' see – tomorrow maybe.

BLOSSOM TIME

It comes round again, and who in the whole
of this half-done world isn't wet
between the mind's legs
with the woods-mulched garlic, bum-fluff greens
and these undomesticating bombs of sunflesh,
here today, gone
with the clichés of the haiku boys?

Cherry white, cherry pink, the snow winds'
ambush, every April of my life
you've sung me into May,
and every April I've ached
for the time and the chutzpah
to sift among the blown petals of speech
for the phonemes to shape you a bowl of praise.

But always I've been busy, always too fussed
with defrosting the fridge, or
the comet-of-a-lifetime . . .
And they're gone, the blossoms,
gone in a night, before the ice in my fridge
has turned to slush . . .

And ah well, I've said, there's always
again, and when the weather's right
I'll iamble a bit, and sit on a stone
and take purposeful note . . .

The late snows are melting on Carreg y Fan,
and again is here: blossoms out, shirts off,
the first legs of the year
driving both shirted and shirtless wild . . .
and – what's this? – the alleged poet
is busier than a busted bee
exercising the goldfish?

This April the blossoms have been saying to me:
'What kind, *gwboi*, what kind
of a presumptuous, nervy bastard are you
that you dare to dream
you'll be present here in a year's turning
– for yet again your pen to ignore us?
Live the now, boy blossom, and finish
your sentence.'

And they unbury for the baby
a morning perhaps or an afternoon
when I gazed from my pram
on a quilted great arc of flouncy sky –
the pink of it, the blue, the necessary crow.

But nothing done, for the forty-seventh time.
And all I dare say, as the storm-troops drive
the last of the lost into the sea, is
'Same time next year?'

UNLEAVING

From floor thirteen, I look
down through the beeches, all but

winnowed, to a black man
posing there for a photo:

as a puff of leaves drifts down
around his head he

stoops to touch, to rustle
the rustling, and then he stands,

brushes each palm, freezes a moment
for the lens to receive him,

unlocks and shuffles on,
two pictures taken.

FORTY-EIGHT AND A HALF

Here I am, Dad, this is the month
I overtake you. Let's do it on horses,
you on my mother's black-maned mare, me astride
the grand if mildly delinquent bay (whose bones are
where now, whose teeth and tail?). I'm coming up
on the outside, Dad, only a stumble can stop me now,
and no flogging of a corpsed cayuse can keep you ahead.

Foxhunting Taff with a penchant for the shires,
you had your Scotch and Three Nuns, your loud afraid laughter
warmed a place you were public schooled not to understand.
But when nights were nights and seasons knew their place
you made a harnessed pony of our lives, her fulfilled leather
creaking with sunlight, as taut as taut words
in the right abode. Then things went, metaphorically speaking,
all to fuck and boarding school buggery, the dreamplate
departed Mum's hand, missed your head and broke
a family's heart: too much horseflesh, too little love.

There were furlongs between us. To your Brylcreemed mohawk,
the revenge of tresses sufficient to thatch
an army of Guevaras; to the alleged music of Sir Harry Lauder,
the orgasmitudes of Hendrix. I didn't want to be a farmer, Dad.

But, neck and neck, through the months of your heart's
perplexed liberation, we found forgiveness, found in each other
the boy and the man, a stander of rounds
to your interrogative sea-lost eyes.
It wasn't long, dark horse, before you cantered free
on the prairies of night: did my brother not tell you
of the sweet one-nighter who declared him at dawn
nearly as good as his dad inside her?

Night, though, had another plan: the black wart that was not,
to which you took an agricultural knife, sporing

45

cancer through every field of your liberated land.
It was daylight, scorched-earth robbery.
The Old Pilferer's taking his time with me: the odd
tooth ripped off, half an acre of topmost turf purloined,
and a heart, like yours, in laconic turmoil.

So here I come, Dad, after twenty-seven years
the plashy nostrils of my lathered mount are panting down
your skeletal neck, you'll be lost any second
in flying hoof-scoops of earth and grass – unless, unless,
yes, c'mon, gimme your hand, I gotcha: leap!
Cwtsh up, Dad, cwtsh up behind me, we'll ride on together
in galloping tandem, my daughters will sing for you, we'll
raise a few rooks from the beech-tops yet;
so put baccy in your pipe and pass me the Teacher's,
there be horizontal times ahead.

'IS THAT WHERE THEY MAKE THE CLOUDS, DAD?'

It is beautiful, the filth gusting
from a stack at Baglan, turned by late sun
to a wing of silver
rising against
the blackly green, languorous hills;
beyond the great dapplers bundling east,
an unearthly simplicity of open sky;
here at our feet the tide bangs in,
loud lengths of it slapping
the concrete steps.
There could be rain. There will be night.

POEM AT A MARRIAGE'S END

You came to me in a dream last night
(strictly, no doubt, without your permission),
yesterday's talons of insulted desire
unfurling for us now siroccan arpeggios,
and it   was like new   impossible times.
From a dream within the dream you woke me:
gone from us, gone the hooks and shrapnel,
we were in airy danger, eye to easefully neutered eye,
of floating clean away from that candled isle.

Here though on earth, where the 'I's won't rhyme,
the windows had fallen out of my face,
a rat had eaten your primroses;
and if we've survived perhaps
a hurricane, there are certain things
blown and broken that can't get fixed,
not by daughters' dreams nor the fumblings of a poem.
And the tears, unto snot, heave also from me.

Three babies a second are born,
two babies a second die. Who hasn't nuzzled
the yeasty hayfield of his baby's head
and studied through brine
all the griefs of history
wobbling there on those podgy shoulders?
Who would choose, at that altar,
to increase by an inch the acres of pain?
But Liberty and Mercy, unhappiest of couples,
can't for long share even a king-size bed.
Now Mercy's lone subterranean moan
has taken ripped red flight,
and my name in many ears is a malediction.

It's twenty years since I wrote you
(tired long since of the verse-fodder role)

a functioning poem:
To not nor from: only in motion!
(and weary doubtless of dodgy exclamations).
I ask for nothing, make offering only
of this scrawny effort
to wish zephyrs on your house
and presence, especially when the buzzard reels,
of strung walls of song and the remnant of a god

who'll see you home at last, if not to heaven.

GRAVITY

I, who moved on earth,
moved on earth like you
through the lower sky,

seemed to have been forgotten
by the bridges I once relied on
to transport me home,

took dangerous flight

and found myself abed
one undark night
on the silvery roof
of a jumbo sailing west,

clinging for splayed life
to the port lintels.

It was cold, loud and drafty,
but I'd been provided
with a blanket or two,
and was perhaps
not always alone.

All night as I dreamed
of falling asleep
I'd jolt to just in time
to jerk back on board
my earth-inclined legs,

finding myself on each occasion

insufficiently afraid.

AN UNCLE'S SATISFACTION°

I want, Tom, my twenty pounds,
and spare me, please, the rebound
that, pissed then, you've no recall –
it just ain't believable:
like too much of what you say,
mere smile beguiling wordplay
or hammed affront – as when I
groaned 'Loan? You mean a bye-bye.'
Though twenty quid's no big thing,
it isn't all that's missing.
We want, *gwboi*, to rescue
what's left of you that rings true.

Beautiful still, my *brawd*'s son,
my girls' cousin of cousins –
your life awaits your arrival,
but it can't, Tom, survive all
the glee-gobbed and woozy bane
of this chronic holiday.
Still the party's boy of boys,
you are heartbeat's overjoy,
ear-tucked fag 'neath Burberry,
jiving hot galactic eyes
and unschooled intelligence
reeking, still, of future tense.
You're wanted on the dancefloor,
not shrinking to some bar bore,
the saloon's lord of earbash,
generous with your father's cash,
taxiing from deal to bar,
cadgerdom's fly superstar.

Tom, you're loved and I'm afraid.
The Unreal Arms's barmaid
has a cliché of a plan
for the boys of Neverland.

51

Sickness, madness, prison, death:
you, before your thirtieth,
could fall through lush vortices
to one, two or more of these –
unless, Tom, an inner tide
can turn against this lifeslide.
Turn, then, those too ready fists
to hands that are harmonists;
that calculating deal-head
to thought's daring fountainhead;
and that lone heart so self-twined
to a re-peopled turbine.

You won't like this poem, Tom,
that sees into your maelstrom
yet fails in its forensic
to feed you an easy fix.
You alone can help yourself,
not some uncle's bardic bombshell.
I want, yes, satisfaction,
a debt that's paid and not shunned,
proof, Tom, you've not given in:
you owe your life its living.

A BODY OF QUESTIONS°

What would seem to be the matter?

★

If our blood distinctly remembers the sea
what vague recollections of supernovae
dwell within our atoms?

★

So these cells got together
and invited you
to make yourself at home?

★

Is there anything more ambitious than a cell?

★

If we all start as women
what is it
that makes me a man?

★

Do we think because we learned to smell?

★

For how long have you inspired the sky?

★

Where precisely have you been
the last six million years?

★

Just looking, eh?

★

Don't you, as you
blink out from the boneroom,
don't you change it all?

★

Do we ever forget – tee tum, tee tum –
the warm symphonies of the womb?

★

Why not be naked and unashamed?

★

Can you feel your chemicals touching each other?

★

If the heart's so full of love
how does it find room for the blood?

★

Who can resist the Islets of Langerhans?

★

How far from the mouths of our caves
do you reckon we've parked our cars?

★

What do they make of all this Space Age food,
our Stone Age stomachs?

★

Is happiness simply the absence of pain?

★

Is hell the pain
we know we cause others?

★

Will the wave be loved, the flesh pleasured?

★

Do you, wet skeleton,
do you play hearts?

★

Have we taken the Earth
and lost the Sky?

★

But listen in your blood
to the song of our sphere:
aren't you too an astronaut?

★

If it weren't for touch
and its addictive delights
where in all Creation would we be?

★

When the heart was set in place
somewhat closer to the loins than the brain
did a smile cross the celestial lips?

★

With so much salt
in our blood, urine, tears, flesh
is it any wonder when lovers kiss
that oceans collide?

★

Fishy, eh?

★

His nine, her ten holes,
the perfect leather coat:
aren't you touched?

★

One of life's little
solitary pleasures, uh?
uh? uh?

★

Don't you feel, enquired the tooth,
that death keeps taking
little bits of you?

★

Is it lonely down there at the big toe,
such a long, cold way from the capital?

★

Is not the harvesting of light
the only work that really matters?

★

Wouldn't you get a better view
of the icebergs of Antarctica
or the lover you've lost
if you closed your eyes?

★

For how much longer,
as we breathe out,
will the trees breathe in?

★

Was not that expression
on your grandson's face
your great-grandfather
taking a walk through him?

★

Is there anything that DNA doesn't know?

★

Is food a matter of time?

★

How many deaths
– spiders, pigs, worms, flies –
have you notched up today?

★

If the cells you're made of
replace themselves every few years

how much younger, do you reckon,
is your body than you?

★

Do you think we've been visited?

★

Can you hear it –
one universe ending, the next beginning:
God's stately heartbeat?

★

Who'd've imagined
that the ear, assailed by molecules of air,
could deliver such open-heart surgery?

★

Whence this addiction,
this ferocious addiction
to the private ownership
of individuals?

*

Doncha find a sneeze out of season
as holy as the tickle
of healing wounds?

*

Is it not a return
to the unhurting dark
from which we came?

*

Would there be, without death, a single poem?

*

Has there ever been
an obligate aerobe
with so many questions?

AND

'Kath' perhaps and 'Crow' maybe – two
names in the sand at half-past midnight
when I step down from the city
to take a leak upon the strand.

A rushed and perchance exuberant script
on a slate washed clean
by the vanished tide,
two longish extra lines unreadable,

but precise too: 29 Jan, 9.35 p.m.

Though many a tide has turned
in much less than three hours,
I wish all lovers well
and dedicate the pleasure
of this piss to them,
Kath perhaps and Crow maybe,

where the sea meets the city,
the orange lights an incoming dark.

POEM FOR ANDIE

On the day, the sudden day in a lover's life
that is like no other, the first beyond
the ending of it all,
you took time to save a Welshman
from the Swiss monsoon,
showed me Basel, showed me bars,
even tried your damnedest to get me a pint
(an army of thimbles had to serve instead).
Though as always at such times
the shades of first days were knocking at your door,
you were bruised but smiling,
could laugh at the rain, the cascades
cascading, threatening to shred the bar's canvas
(while this elder statesman of Welsh windcraft
wished himself, in vain, twenty years younger).

So *proscht*, *iechyd da*, here's a poem of sorts
to the two who lasted three whole years,
this stark day's freedom and the strength to use it.
Life, I know you know,
is no safe-as-Switzerland, blue-eyed fountain,
but a Rhine of a river,
and we go with what's gone
towards the who, what, when,
the glorious ambush
of what sometimes it hurts to lose,
(it's raining again) the fountain moments.

'A LAS CINCO DE LA TARDE'[10]
OR 'LIFE IS NOT A STROLL ACROSS A FIELD'
(Pasternak)

(for Margot)

It was five, exactly five in the afternoon
but I was too foozled with grassy reefer
and summery love to heed the clockwise cry
of yon buzzard prof. of Spanish lit.:
the farmboy would take his city girl
on a stroll across a hilltop field,
its dandelions, its harmless cows.
Seventy or so innocuously nosey
black-n-white droolers snortily circled till I
batted them away
with a whoop and seasoned farmerish wave.
I wuz az high az dem mooz wuz crazy:
my whirligig arms stirring ever faster
a gargantuan cup of Friesian tea.
It was five, yes, five in the afternoon
when professor buzzard, reeling on high,
decided to remind a deafened ear
of the twentieth century's number one word, 'b', 'u', 't' . . .
And at five o'clock, as the lover and his lass
were most of the way across that field
the bovine circle halted before us
and turned at once
into a straight and panting, asthmatic line,
a cohort of incontinent moos–at–arms
with not so much as a horn between them,
no, not a horn, but, *madre mia,*
through the end of that nose, o what a ring!
and o what a burning in that field marshal's eye
of pristine murder, immaculate rape.
Women and children first, MarGOt!

But is it run or is it walk?
Is it butt or is it gore?
Head sunk at the ready, snorted breaths
stamping the grass, he permitted his playthings
an elephant's lifetime to reach and scale
that gate of barbed exquisite wire.
'I'll be back,' he mooed, 'I'll be
back one day, fences or no . . .'
One day, butty bull, doubtless you will,
but for now it's steak *au poivre* to you.

'FORSAKING ALL OTHERS'

It came to her one evening of *boeuf en croûte*
that if once perhaps she had been in love
she'd been in love with love and the idea
of a man – not the man himself, even then,

whom she sits with now,
a couple among largely silent couples,
eating dead animals and gazing at the sea.

IDEAL HOMES

Where all, for moneyed miles, have phones,
a phone, in an empty kiosk, rings,
it rings and it rings.
I cycle on by, deliver my deliveries,
then cycle back
past the empty but now silent kiosk
and past also, dragging her beauty
away from that silence,
heeled and furred,
a creature wrapped in tears.

MANNES IOYE

Blissfully blissful and two
lovely kids, no
language please
in front of the ladies . . .

He's lunching under lilac,
his lady wife
away for the week,

couldn't live now
without her
nor imagine life
if she
were unfaithful, not
that she would be.
Woman is mannes Ioye and ál his blis.

She's away for the week.
One more pint
then it's down to the beach
to take in the totty,
after that maybe
a ride into town,
the new massage parlour,
five quid your back,
ten the front
and twenty for 'relief'.
The big F itself is
not for sale
and anyway who
wants to risk disease?
How then on earth
could he break the bad news?

Unfaithful? No . . .
He couldn't tell her of course
– emotions and things – she
wouldn't understand,
but blissfully blissful and wanting
for nothing,
not in all the world,

save relief now and then
from a hired hand.

IN VINO

Four thousand miles and three years later
the two that were
sit breathing together
in the one room,

    in Canada she
    in Wales he
    whereas in the States you see . . .

damp pathetic squib of a meeting,
a lesson in geography
with adventitious reference
to aphasic linguistics.

The winos next door,
blurting it all all the time,
are true neighbours:
    'I'll tell you one thing you
    goddam nogood son of a bitch you
    haven't got the guts of a fuckin mouse.'

Our words forget us
and we pussyfoot in eggskin shoes,
I can no longer read
a smile's edging,
your practised hands perplex me.

    'I know you're in there you
    lowly degraded cock-sucker
    you're in there suckin cunts you prick.'

Between the two houses
a lush on crutches
hurls all morning
cock-fearing cunt-hating cannibal words

to someone inside,
then he gives up and goes in
from the weather.

I'd be afraid now even to
touch your arm.

BEAUTIFUL STRANGERS

In the sun-shafted gloom
of the Joiners Arms, I
seem to read

and she across the room
studiously sips,
avoiding the gaze of yon
shaggy slurper . . .

until, that is,
a second solo beauty
swans in
diffracting starlight,

and I receive, I notice,
her undivided attention.

PUNCTUATION POEMS

;

SEMICOLON

Cwtsh up, o dread-struck,
to the jinxed, the best avoided,
the point that panics;
I will not, if you come to know me,
dement or destroy you.

I am the point of balance,
a glass of iced water
at the half-way hotel.

It could all end here, yes –
but it doesn't; there's more and maybe
better to come.

COLON

If, these days, I play less than second fiddle
to that single-minded stopper of every show,

I am popular still where appetites
have expectations – the Americans adore me:

I promise and – old stager – I deliver.
I have ambitions for us all; but one for myself –

to bridge my divide and become as one –
is a future it might prove unwise to explore.

,

COMMA

Bourgeois, you say?
Managerial, I'd prefer:
everywhere at once,
fit and vigilant,
sorting, dividing, clarifying,

and master of the inspirations.

What happens in the end
is no business of mine:
I'm engaged to ensure
that things proceed –

though in the fog that descends
when lawyers decide
I've got out of hand
I may be the maker of mighty trouble.

DASH

I am – you've noticed – the great
disruptor: there's a violence in me
that can stem – at a stroke –
a river's flow.

Mistake me not
for the frenzied penman's
dash-of-all-trades
nor for my wee, hyphenating cousin.
I may seem, sometimes, a cheery joiner

but disconnection if not erasure's
my line. I have only to unite
– nineteen-forty-nine DASH –
your first date with your last

to write you out.

Though it may please you all
to call me dash,
I am not, if need be,
incapable of patience.

HYPHEN

Let's be friends, if not lovers.

If wars have blundered
across my bridgework,
so too, in time,
have the treaties had to teeter.

Let the swaggering dash
go loudly about his disruptive game.
I, at half the size,
am the line that combines –

though not for me, fear not,
exclusive matrimonial rights.
I comprehend the atom's
binding repulsions,
the together that remains
a free-breathing twain.

‘ ’

INVERTED COMMAS

A twosome, always,
untouching yet inseparable,
like a marriage gone to speechless seed.

We raise curtains, sound fanfares,
and seal, when all's said, the silences.

We have, ourselves, nothing to say,
one loneliness turned in upon the other,

and mocked by soixante-neuf's mirage.

,

APOSTROPHE

The unbuttoner, maybe, the relâchez-vous.
Get me right, though, before you're seventeen,
or be haunted for life
by cabbage's, potato's, spud's 'n' pear's.

I prow, yes, the absences,
my presence proof,
when I'm found where I belong,

of something missing, something possessed.

● ● ●

ELLIPSIS

If you're inclined
not to notice
the . . . gusting
from that stack among the pines,

then for you, blithe waltzer,

I am footsteps eternal
in everlasting snow . . .

!

EXCLAMATION MARK

Sexy! Real! Hilarious! New!
I rear tumescent
from flaccid horizons,
spinmaestro of spectral thrills.

I'm the short cut
to a cul-de-sac
that's painted to look like
the heart's highway.

Don't even think of
loneliness! age! poverty! death!

I

ITALICS

Look at me. I said *look at me.*
That's more like it.
Where there is weakness, you see,
I swagger into power.

I have only, yearning rightward,
to raise my voice

for all, fore and aft,
to declare their undying
insignificance.

And if, sometimes, I'm obliged
to *SHOUT*, it's then, maybe,
that a little light fascism
comes into play.

●

FULL STOP

Whatever in life
is muddled, side-stepped, misconstrued
there is no ignoring me,
full stop, new sentence.
And should that sentence prove
too painfully long
you have only to invoke
my easeful abbreviatory skills,
full stop, new par.

Whichever way you wind –
via colons of plenty, dashes of joy –
I will oblige you, ready or not,
with your vanishing point.

HAIKU AND SENRYU

we do not see

til flight tilts them sunward –

oystercatchers

how many of the dead,

as I climb these old stairs,

do I pass coming down

kept awake

by her sleepless

yawns

from nowhere, this hot

afternoon, a moan of wind,

the rattle of a can

sky that seems blue;

this married man who

seems to be smiling

have I learned –

since last I heard the buzzard's

day-long cry – nothing?

winos a–tiptoe

on midday streets, trying

not to wake us

only the blind man sees

that the leaf we're handing round

is a maple

an escaped balloon

sails up past my window

pursued by wailing

windy demo –

swatted in the face

by a 'Peace' flag

high tide after the storm,

the bay bobbing with

bits of forest

the lipsticked wineglass –

re-filled, by sunrise, with

rainwater

September barbie –

when it begins again

'to get late early'

on their backs,

the two plastic chairs

in a swirl of leaves

I open the window –

dogs barking in the nights

of childhood

sunlight sliding

down and up a spider's

invisible rope

                              hill-top graves –

                              their headstones catching

                              the last of the light

leaves snowing

through the brazen blue,

and countable on trees

the barmaid I once

craved – creased now, like me,

and double-chinned

from the ice-rubbled

foreshore, twenty pale chunks

detach themselves and fly

hooter booms –

and a slice of the city

sails into the night

BORDERS

What begins for you
where the waves break
– sea or land, land or sky –

depends on where
you're coming from, depends
on where you're going to

and whether you
have legs or fins, lungs or gills.

'£23 WILL SAVE A LIFE'

So we send forty-six.

We do not send
ninety-two
or a hundred and eighty-four.

We buy the kids an ice cream,
ourselves another bottle of wine.

FLYLEAF

On the window glass
the amble of a fly;

outside on the grass
the tremble of a leaf:

there's just time for the fly
to step over the leaf

before they vanish both.

HERE, NOW

Venus in the blue
dancing on the tide
with a sliver of moon . . .

and on the sea wall, with beer,
a gathering of atoms
talking about it all.

FORCE TEN

We'd seen it coming but we held
to the sailing: how the dust
had twirled, how the gusted olives
turned bellies of tin to a snuffed-out sky.

We had a choice. Now this ship
full of glasses and carpet and light
bumps us through the storm. We abandon
plates, go early to our berths, trusting all
to the wisdom of metres and dials,

trading tonight's just possible risk
for the blatant disasters of dream.

BOURBON STREET

Every evening, after rain, the lovetrees
drip from French white verandahs,
champagnes of mimosa
escape to an absent Delta sky.
And every evening, as lovebirds high
in their cages sing, the street
redresses, the men who sell her
slouch down through her yawning
to call and hawk her with glee faces,
their heels beating time on her cobbles of glass.

At her restless blue doorways
the eyes hunger, yearning through smoke
and the hammerings of strobe
for the syrup, the naked flesh of dance.

On uppers, on downers, in these yards
dank with memory of slaves,
her body, blindfold, spreads for hot eyes
the dream they have paid for, the liquid
their thirsts will never reach.
        *And remember, honey − when you
        catch in your mirror the whites of his eyes,
        when you hear the jerk groan, put your
        hand in his pocket.*

Cold lips at her ear
dance her all night to the dollar's tune:
there are no more strings
to the bluesman's guitar, no words any more
in the singer's mouth.

Through the emptying bars
a grey first light pushes its broom.
Men soft as babies, their fingers drying

round the necks of bottles,
sail from her doorways, stumbling,
as they go, on the sleep of beggars.

The dawn TVs
lull her to bed, hungry
for her dreams. Eyes close, mouth
drops open: and in they glide, Messrs.
Bullshit and Shoeshine, and out again
they make their way.
She dreams of food, and wakes each day
to find her jaw collapsed,
her mouth rolling with broken teeth.

Elsewhere, each morning,
Bullshit and Shoeshine report with the goods.

TRANSLATIONS
MOSTLY

THE CUCUMBERS OF WOLVERHAMPTON

[from the Welsh of Ifor ap Glyn]

I've made this alarming discovery –
it's been like a blow to the ear:
the cucumbers of Wolverhampton
are Welsher than people round here!

It's something I saw in the paper,
I could hardly believe my eyes,
but there it was in black and white –
and *The Sun* don't tell no lies.

I was thumbing around in all innocence
between the racing and the Page Three pets,
when I saw in this piece that our bodies
are nothing but chemistry sets!

Giblets and bones are what's inside me,
I'd believed until that day –
not calcium, potassium,
carbon and water –
even iron, so they say.

True love may well be likened to steel,
but there's iron in every man too;
there's iron in the bosom of every woman,
and silicone in the breasts of a few.

Although we're quite rich in iron,
we're seventy per cent water, or more!
(Though why the water doesn't rust the iron,
the scientists aren't quite sure).

We're all H$_2$O, a full seventy per cent!
It's a fact you can't gainsay!
Gallons and gallons of Tryweryn am I
as I slosh along my way.

Now, the people of Bilston and Handsworth
may not sound as Welsh as they oughta,
but they drink what flows from Tryweryn
and they're seventy whole per cent water.

So they're Welsh by pipage, if not
parentage; the census is therefore wrong:
a barrel of Welsh red water
is each Leroy, Singh and Wong.

And so in the Midlands of England
there are ten million lost Welsh others;
isn't it time we pushed the border back east
to embrace our abandoned brothers?

It would solve all our problems with tourists:
they'd be living in Cymru too,
with Powys spreading to Norfolk,
and Gwynedd ending at Crewe.

A great *Sun*-reading brotherhood,
sharing alike both friend and foe.
I don't mind being on a par with the Sais
. . . but second to a vegetable? No!

Because now here comes the downside.
The paper then started to number
the contents of animals, plants and veg –
including the cu-bloody-cumber.

While there's no shortage of water in us,
cucumbers have ninety per cent!
The cucumbers of Wolverhampton
are Welsher than Gwynedd and Gwent.

So if some cheeky blockhead comes along
proclaiming to all in sight
that he's 'more of a Welshman than you',
don't reply 'You looking for a fight?'

Just put on a knowing smile and say,
'That's nothing, stop making a fuss –
the cucumbers of Wolverhampton
are Welsher than every last one of us.'

A ROUND FOR REMSEN°

1. STINGER'S BAR, REMSEN, N.Y.

(for David Lloyd)

Home in, take a bird's or a plane's eye view,
on waters black, the forests after snow
like pubic hair on pale skin,
home in on twilit, one-bar Remsen,
as happy, happy-hourless, as happy gets,
and yes, you bet, a Welsh-made town.
Meet, with Martini, Joy of the woods
whose retirement tales are down to just the one,
– the wild turkeys, the mother hen –
and her cigar of a husband phoning for the cavalry
of a welcome for us, the poets from Wales.
He wants flags, he wants the mayor,
while Joy of the woods wants to tell three strangers
with the cocktail dust of cities upon them
all about this twilight zone, the thirst that no liquid,
and the wild turkeys, they shoot them, you know,
the thirty-five turkeys that took
forever, you wouldn't believe, to cross the road
in front of her car. And the one, the mother
who at gifted moments emerges from the pines
to visit their place, lonely seeming, but not surely
without a mate somewhere, somewhere in the forest
a clutch of young that Joy imagines and has never seen.
We're a long way here off anyone's map,
says Joy of the once Manhattan woods, deep, deep, deep
in the twilight zone, with Waylon and Willie,
Johnny Cash and Jerry Lee, the good ole boys n girls
of brotherly, quietly diasporate Remsen.

2. STINGER'S, REMSEN

[from the Welsh of Menna Elfyn]

('Never shall I give the brother from Liverpool opportunity to close a door against me. He rejoices that the brother from Remsen and his people have done this.' Samuel Roberts (S.R.), Llanbrynmair, in a letter to *Y Cronicl*.)

Closed to us the Meeting House doors, we peeped in like nosy
    sparrows,
spread – brows to pane – a wing against the glass, but caught
scarce a glimpse; light aslant shutting out light, our soles scuffing
a well-thumbed memoir of dirty snow. Cue, then, to seek out
some cosier abode; easier, late in the afternoon, to contend
with shadows beneath a roof. And so, in a bar, we found ourselves
in a fellowship meeting where a verse, once recited, sparked cries
of excitement, a woman's 'From Wales!' husky with smoke and
    welcome;
forgotten the strife of our motherland's winter in that spring
    turned
by those upstate folk into a cantata for our poetry's mission.
'Where's the mayor? Where's the flag?' said a man raising a phone
to his ear and spitting amens, hot and blue, to summon them forth
to the sanctum. The congregation were by now as one, all warmly
new Welsh, boasting pedigrees by the pitcherful:

early spring, it was; every topic unstoppered, a thrill to the throat.

Clouds of witness descend in only two forms: cacophony or calm.
And I felt in the thick of that babbling host a presence within:
of psalms beneath the make-up's grease, and wisdoms laid down
under brows mascaraed thick with fair and unfair weather.
Yes, she slunk towards me, pressed my flesh as if in touch
with the softness of a peach, knowing that only sisters
feel the weight of such things, as if their wombs wept
with vacancy. 'Remsen,' she said, 'is a twilight zone.

Welsh town or not, here there's nothing but ducks
to feed every day as I rise among the morning's tatters.
But they are my friends, my downy ones, my darlings,
and the turkey, O! the one wild turkey . . . who wandered away
into the woods, and will surely hatch soon a brood of her own.'

Twenty, she declaimed, twenty she'd once proudly counted
Zigzagging their way to some gathering somewhere.

Delivered, by now, was the fond afternoon to evening's door,
the cool air outside plump with many a 'Wild Turkey' of her
    breath.

3. NAMES

[from the Welsh of Iwan Llwyd]

The road swings
by Turning Stone
to Rome and to Verona:

names that landed here
from the old continent
way to the east

on the same wind as the wild geese
forming up to fly back to Canada
before they're caught by a late spring:

and, islanded in swells of snow,
the Bethels and Capel Cerrigs,
their names preserved in cold store,

names from one of those distant lands
which are a cross on every stone,
breaking through the white cover:

names lost like the Welsh lost
in Stinger's Bar & Grill,
and yet, in the welcome

to an errant Taff,
the names are still there,
calling for the mayor, for a civic reception,

and the beer and the whisky
flowing with the flow of the homeland songs
and the country songs on the juke box:

and before departing
the 'Twilight Zone' of names,
beyond Rome and Verona,

I counted, one by one, the wild turkeys
turning for home, leaving behind them
footprints in the snow like tiny crosses.

RONCESVALLES

[from the Welsh of Iorwerth C. Peate]

Do you remember, mountains of grey,
    the turmoil lost to long-gone times?
'Those deeds, to us, were but yesterday,
    one of the scented wind's pastimes.
From that voiceless age no soldier tall
will stride through the mist to Roncesvalles.'

Did you see the armies of Charlemagne,
    envoys of the utter nullity of man,
and the glory of France, the pride of Spain,
    Roland and his men, the grand Suleiman?
'They are nothing but mutes, their power spent.
In Roncesvalles what endures yet

is our mountain might, the grass and heather,
    the bells of herds distantly tinking,
and the humble men bending together
    as the knell sounds before sun's sinking.
The stars and the dawn, the mists and the night,
in Roncesvalles are the beacons of might.

Across the valley the darkness spread
    (o! famous men, how brief is fame),
we hear the cattle breathing deep breaths
    (o! life, how small the realm you proclaim);
I wait until the shadow comes to call,
and the night that was, in Roncesvalles.

AIRSTRIP ST ATHAN

[from the Welsh of Iorwerth C. Peate]

God in his wondrous grace a garden did sow
between sea and mountain, whose paths would ease
the wearied people to meadows whence would flow
the waters of Bethesda, Eglwys Brywys's peace.
Many a cheerful village he sprinkled there –
Llan-faes, Aberddawen, Y Fflemin Melyn –
dazzle-white gems in the grasslands' care,
and hedge, lane and dune with tales beyond telling.
But now they're as dust, all passion broken on the wheel –
unhappy man whose wants he cannot quell
turning leisurely roads into highways of steel
that deliver nothing of Llan-dwf's peace or Llangrallo's spell.
 And the gracious Vale, from 'Barry' to 'Porthcawl',
 is raw meat to greedy hell's mechanic sprawl.

DOGS

[from the Welsh of Rhydwen Williams]

The whole of doghood I've seen in my time –
Dogs great, dogs small, dogs comic, dogs godly and good;
Dogs under-arm, dogs under-arse, dogs dull, dogs devoted to
    crime,
Dogs highbrow, dogs a-grovel, dogs dishevelled, dogs a plague in
    flood.
Yes, I've seen and heard the whole canine catalogue,
And I have still in my nostrils the smell of two generations of
    dog.

Well I remember yesteryear's dogs in the long ago Valley –
Funny little old mongrel dogs; dogs of every size and format;
Dogs happy, dogs bereft, dogs that would dog you up any old
    alley,
Dogs fearless of both man and devil – except sometimes the
    devil of a cat!
Carrying messages and cocking legs, the little old dogs of our
    boyhood,
More alive to me now than ever – though gone, a long time
    since, for good.

Of the Mansion and its hounds recollection now stirs –
I was the servant boy, shining shoes, chopping logs, replenishing
    coal,
Mine the joy before breakfast of feeding and grooming those
    loathsome curs,
Unleashing their lusts, giving them a hand to lick, taking them
    for a stroll.
To be lackey to a dog is something most men would rather not,
But set aside the gentry and the stench, and that's the lackey's
    lot.

By dogs I was surrounded from the day that I first saw the light –
Wil Tŷ-Cwrdd's dog and Tomos the Shop's, Gran's dog and the
  dog next door;
And when there'd seem not a hair of the wild menagerie in sight
Suddenly there'd come a woof-beneath-the-bed or an under-
  the-sofa scratching of floor.
A dog might seem a priceless creation, but the truth is, though
  some may find it odd,
That it has in abundance the virtues of Man, the Devil's devisings
  and the omnipresence of God.

The old fellowship by now has more or less come to an end:
Of pedigree companions all that's left to me is just this one,
A lop-eared, amusing dandy of a boy, whom I never have to
  reprehend,
With his back and his legs like hedges, and his bark like the blast
  from a gun.
In an hour or so we'll go out, him and me, have a walkies
  powwow,
The pedigree sign of a bow tie marking the higher-nosed one as
  the bow-wow.

THE SHOULDER OF LAMB

[with a nod to William Carlos Williams]

so much depends
upon

a Welsh sheep's
shoulder

braised with *rhos
Mair*

beside the white
earlies

ENGLYNS

[from the Welsh of Ifor ap Glyn]

Englyns are akin to scampi –
no one's sure exactly what they are,
and you're usually sorry you asked . . .
for anyone who fancies
that he can explain them
is about as engaging
as a talkative bore when you're busting for the bog,
a CSE in biology,
a member of the SDP,
or last week's *TV Times*.

It's in school that many first stumble upon them
. . . along with bullies,
the whiff, in the chem lab, of stew,
and everyone else's hand in the air
when you don't have the faintest clue.

They don't teach much that's useful
to you
in school
like:
how to unfasten a bra;
but they *do* teach you
such invaluable things as
how to deconstruct an englyn.
What's the use of learning how to strip down
the carburettor
when there's nothing more that you'd adore
than a driving lesson
in an englyn afire on cylinders four!

Englyns are not a kind of bratwurst . . .
a bratwurst has no trouble raising laughs . . .
especially if it's a 'stand up' bratwurst.

Englyns can't be compared to dogs.
An englyn will neither give rise to fleas,
nor fetch your new slippers as you take your ease,
it'll simply inform you that the old pair
were so much better than these.

Englyns are also unlike ashtrays;
they can hold things that shine
as well as what's ashen,
and no parlour should be without one
in case a poet should call.

Because englyns are ancient –
A kind of bardic bouncing cheque –
they're like last night's curry, inclined to come back
after fifteen hundred years –
and that can't be bad.

Writing the little devils
is as much as ever a fag,
but things will be somewhat different
when we've englyns that 'boil in the bag'.

I HAVE°

[from the Spanish of Nicolás Guillén]

When I see myself, when I touch myself –
me, yesterday's Johnny-with-Nothing,
and today John-the-Lot,
today the man with it all,
I swivel my eyeballs, I peer,
I see and feel myself
and I ask myself – how could it have happened?

I have now, let's see,
I have now the pleasure of striding my country,
owner of all that lies before me,
gazing right up close at what before I did not have –
mine the sugar harvest,
mine the city,
mine the army,
mine today, now and forever – and yours too, ours
this sweeping refulgence
of ray, star, flower.

I have, let's see,
I have now the pleasure –
me, peasant, worker, 'ordinary man' –
I have the pleasure, for instance,
of entering a bank
and talking to the manager,
not in English,
not in 'yes sirs' and 'no sirs',
but talking to him straight, in Spanish,
as *compañero* . . .

I have now, let's see,
the freedom at last (being a black man)
to enter unhindered
a dance hall or a bar.

And no one in a hotel reception
can shout that they don't have room for me,
just a small room, not a swanky great suite,
a small room to lay my head in.

I have, let's see,
the sweet lack of rural police
catching me and jailing me,
bursting in to turf me off my land, out onto
the crown of the highway.
I have my having of the land as my having of the sea,
no country club,
no high-life,
no tennis and no yacht,
but from beach to beach, from wave to wave
an open blue democratic giant,
the sea, no less.

I have, let's see,
my having learned to read
my having learned to count,
my having learned already to
write, think, laugh . . .

I have, let's see, on top of what I have,
a place to work,
a place to learn,
a little something to eat.
I have, let's see,
I have, quite simply, what I had to have.

ADVICE TO A YOUNG POET°

It is a journey towards the unknown.
Perhaps your only clue is the Saharan dust
that ghosts, at dawn, the paintwork of your car.

There'll be camels en route and kif and jellabahs,
but the place you arrive at
will be quite other than you could have foreseen,

and you too will not be unchanged.

★

It has to do with beginnings,
it has to do powerfully (weak word)
with the rearing force that seeded you,
and with the unimportant, vital shards
that you've plucked from the stubble
and that you will not yield
to the oblivion

about which
it has also to do.

★

Know language, know languages, know
your own language, that you may take words
beyond words: a poetry

of leaps.

★

To serve the poem
you will need to be
in a devotional trance;

cast a spell perhaps
with music or a walk or a stern espresso,
then savour the occasion
of pulling up a chair
to the making table;
savour the paper, savour the pen;
raise a glass, if you like,
– of water, coldest water –
to the planet and this life,
blow the muse a hopeful kiss

and write.

★

May your night be sleepless
until you are at least on speaking terms
with the stranger-word you met today.

★

If you despair
that no word
can do more than fumble
at the reality of a wave,

take heart
from the oceanic force
that churns in the space

between word and word.

★

Words of all kinds
have their uses,
but don't forget the power

of little words – the 'then' twiced
that brings a bitter *hiraeth* home;
the abstracting 'and' that makes such music
of 'a little tiny boy'.

Be sparing, though,
of one small, one-letter word
that's often too big for its own boasts.

*

There are some words
so 'ensorcellingly' (for instance)
full of themselves
that you'd best not use them
more than once
in an entire book

– if not in the whole of a writing life.

*

You will be instructed,
container of multitudes,
to get a voice, just one voice,
and, having got it, to superglue
that priceless commodity
to your bardic being.

Ignore such calls
to monovocal bliss.
Listen, instead, to the wayward voice
of each new poem.

Many poems. Many voices.

*

Avoid the poetic:
the typeface designed by garden gnomes;
the bespoke poesy
of words like 'forlorn', 'myriad', 'russet';
cheap 'n' easy lists of plants and things
with fabulous names;
the routine molestation of innocent nouns
by posses of pervert adjectives;
p p p p p p p p p p p p p p p p pseudo-
experimental party turns
designed to impress;
sub-Dylanesque word heaps
designed to impress;
sandyfloss confections like
'the parrot of his confusion' and 'the lumbago of her doom';
waffly abstractions lost in space;
rhymes that only rhyme;
lists like this.

Your aim should be
not fog and tricks
but accuracy and magic.

★

Do not expect a slap-on
of numerology, tarot
and recycled hocus-pocus
to conjure up the magic –

it will come, if it comes,
through the arteries of speech.

★

Wait, after the latest
tanker disaster,

before wading in
with an ireful ode

that does nothing but add
to the poetry slick.

*

The tree improvers, who thought themselves
poet, demolished the willow

that graced the entrance
to the graceless building, replacing the tree
with a branchy installation

unloved by all.

There are times when a poet
should do precisely nothing

except let trees speak for themselves.

*

Go for a pint, now and then, with Dr Williams
– or Herr Brecht, Monsieur Rimbaud, Señor Neruda.

until, with his book on your knee
in the rumourous bar,

you get to know him on first-name terms;
he may even, before the night's out,
buy you a pint.

*

Attend, keep note:
you may not remember
in a day's time, let alone a year's,

this morning's red admiral
lowering, after rain, onto steaming slate –

unless you break from kissing
to write it down.

★

Praise, by all means,
the luscious drama of locking tongues,

but honour too the everyday,
and do not neglect your dreams.

★

Though a good critic could save
your poetry's soul, beware resentful destructors
and the scientising jargoneers.

Your adviser too –
he may be semi-toothless and scraggy of pate,
but he too has a frightening amount
still to learn.

★

Don't be cowed by a brush
with anyone's canon.

★

Poems, *au contraire* – and not least in Cymru –
have made many things happen.

Word surgeons, speech architects:
poets are among
the language animal's makers of life.

★

Sing for Wales, sure, but don't shut your trap
on all the rest – it ain't crap.

★

The straight thrust, lethally honed,
may cause, on occasion, creative offence;

but for memorable action,

slantwise is wiser,
as is out from behind
who knows what bushes.

★

Don't spend too much time
drunk/in bed/doped/watching TV/
waiting for the *awen*.

You haven't got long:
only, if you're lucky,
some 300,000 wakeful hours

– and the art school dance
is already long past.

★

Even in cold, unpromising weather
keep the door at least ajar –
encourage visitation.

Tick over, perhaps,
by transcribing a dream,
baking bread
or translating someone else's lines

until that moment, sooner or later,
of groin-tingling ambush.

★

'The poet must know everything,'
Hugh MacDiarmid forgot to say
that Rilke said.

★

It may sometimes be there,

but here is rarely
too small a place.

★

Know your place – its rocks, its soils,
the movement of its waters –
not only by maps and histories
but by body and residential mind.

Walk it, eat from it, drink its rain,
ask among its breezes
for sign and sound
of those who filled their lungs here
when the mammoth roamed
or when coal was a possibility of trees –

dis-cover your community.

★

Know your place. What legends and myths
have had their shaping here?
What stories, novels, histories?
And who have been denied a voice?

What songs, here,
await their singing?

And how, in this place, worker of the word,
might you make yourself useful?

★

Know your times.

Who's got the food?
Who's got the money?
Who's got the water?
Who wants the oil?
Who's got the bombs?

And as you, lucky winner, flush
your piss away with drinking water,
you might ask yourself
what a poem might need to do
to imagine a tomorrow.

★

It is a music.

★

If you're afraid they'll call it prose
then that is their pedantic problem:
if what you have written
does what you want it to do

(and a little more),
then it's in with a chance –

let it loose

to go about, if it can,
its business in the world.

★

The poem, remember, has consequences,
is a made, additional earthly presence:
what you say (and more) will be what it does –

and lives,
if only in infinitesimal ways,
may never be the same.

★

Don't content yourself
with those clouds skating the water's calm:

be wise to the weeds,
the fish unfathomed.

★

Having come down firmly
in favour of snow,

think instead

coal.

★

Delight, of course,
in the play and shapeshift
of this serious game,

but don't flinch from asking
of your new-born creation

'Who needs it?'

★

Bear in mind, as you write,
that this poem

could be your last.

★

You may have, from the outset,
your creation's last line,

but a poem's ending is not its end.

NOTES ON THE POEMS

HOTEL GWALES (p. 24)
The poem alludes to an episode in 'Branwen ferch Llŷr' in *The Mabinogion*, in which seven warriors, who have returned from the campaign in Ireland, live on the island of Gwales (or Grassholm) off the western coast of Pembrokeshire, without ageing or any recollection of their former grief and pain – until one of them disobeys an injunction not to open 'the Cornwall-facing door'. Brad Mehldau is an American jazz pianist. 'Gwales' is pronounced 'GWAH-less'.

SOME LINES TO REQUEST POTEEN (p. 25)
The form of this poem, like that of 'An Uncle's Satisfaction', is an adaptation of a traditional Welsh poem of request, using aspects of the *cywydd* metre, namely lines of seven syllables, arranged in couplets, the accentuation of whose end-rhymes alternates between the lines' final and penultimate syllables. *Heddlu* is Welsh for police. The Welsh poetic tradition of *Cynghanedd* (lit. 'harmony'), based on complex alliterative patterns and internal rhymes, is described in the *Princeton Encyclopedia of Poetry and Poetics* (1993) as 'the most sophisticated system of poetic sound-patterning practised in any poetry in the world'. Very few poets, including this one, have had any success replicating its effects in English. *Sláinte* and *iechyd da* mean cheers or good health in Irish and Welsh respectively. *Awen* means muse.

ON THE EDUCATION OF WELSH BUS DRIVERS (p. 29)
Demetia was the realm of the Iron-Age tribe inhabiting south-west Wales during the Roman occupation. *Haelionus* means generous.

LLYWELYN AP GRUFFUDD FYCHAN (p. 31)
Llywelyn ap Gruffudd Fychan, of Caeo in Carmarthenshire, was a prosperous landowner and supporter of Owain Glyndŵr, who was press-ganged by Henry IV into helping him find Glyndŵr's base. Llywelyn led Henry and his army on a wild goose chase, enabling Owain to escape to Gwynedd. Realizing that he had

been duped, Henry had Llywelyn publicly disembowelled and dismembered in front of the castle gates at Llandovery on October 9, 1401. This poem was commissioned for the unveiling of a memorial to Llywelyn at Llandovery on October 6, 2001. The *uchelwyr* were the indigenous land-owning class.

'ROLL ON, THOU DEEP AND DARK BLUE OCEAN, ROLL!' (p. 33)
This quotation, from Byron's *Childe Harold* (canto IV, stanza 179) continues: 'Ten thousand fleets sweep over thee in vain; / Man marks the earth with ruin – his control / Stops with the shore.'

ONCE UPON A TIME (p. 41)
The poem refers to reading the tragic story of 'Branwen ferch Llŷr' in *The Mabinogion*. See the note to 'Hotel Gwales'.

AN UNCLE'S SATISFACTION (p. 51)
For a description of the form of this poem, see the note for 'Some Lines to Request Poteen'.

A BODY OF QUESTIONS (p. 53)
These questions, bereft for the most part of rational answers, resulted from a commission from the Princess of Wales Hospital, Bridgend for some poems on the theme of the human body, for a glass artwork in the hospital's foyer. Designed by the Swansea glass artist David Pearl, the artwork incorporated versions – some of them translated into Welsh by Menna Elfyn – of about sixteen of these questions.

'A LAS CINCO DE LA TARDE' (p. 62)
'A las cinquo de la tarde' (at five o'clock in the afternoon) is the percussive and ominous refrain that rings through Federico Garcia Lorca's famous lament for the bullfighter Ignacio Sánchez Mejías.

A ROUND FOR REMSEN (p. 102)
Remsen is a small, one-bar town founded by the Welsh (without the bar) in upper New York State in the mid-nineteenth

century. Menna Elfyn, Iwan Llwyd and I, on a reading tour of the States in 1997, stayed in Syracuse, NY with the poet David Lloyd and his wife, the sculptor Kim Waale. David drove us out to the snowy farmlands north of Utica where the most conspicuous insignia of Welsh settlement was a scattering of solitary clapboard chapels, their graveyards full of Evanses and Joneses, and the Welsh dragon fluttering proudly outside the occasional farmstead. It was more or less by chance (and thirst) that we ended up in Remsen where, after viewing the town's typically Welsh, and beautifully preserved, stone-built chapel, we found our way to Stinger's Bar & Grill. Such was the welcome lavished on us, when they realised we were from Wales, that we'd probably be there still, had we discovered Remsen at the end rather than at the beginning of our tour. We later wrote poems about our Remsen afternoon, and I translated those of Menna and Iwan.

I HAVE (p. 113)
Translated with Humberto Gatica.

ADVICE TO A YOUNG POET (p. 115)
This sequence is a response, to some extent, to Harri Webb's short – and in some quarters infamous – poem 'Advice to a young poet', which reads in full: 'Sing for Wales or shut your trap / All the rest's a load of crap.' (Meic Stephens (ed.), *Harri Webb: Collected Poems*, Gomer Press, 1995). *Hiraeth* is one of those famously 'untranslatable' Welsh words meaning, roughly, 'longing'. I owe the observation on Shakespeare's song-lyric 'When that I was *and* a little tiny boy' (to be found in both *King Lear* and *Twelfth Night*) to the poet and indispensable critic Tony Conran. *Awen* means Muse.